HOW TO LEAVE LONDON

How to Leave London

Alex Bagner & Seth Carnill

HOXTON MINI PRESS

ALEX BAGNER is a writer, an editor and, more recently, an innkeeper. Over her career she has been the Design Editor of *Wallpaper** magazine and the Head of Content at onefinestay and has worked with brands including Goodwood, N Family Club and Harvey Nichols. In 2017, she and her husband Christopher fulfilled a lifelong dream by opening The Rose, a handsome hotel, bar and restaurant in Deal, Kent. They left London with their children a couple of years later, and are now living by the sea just up the road from their new venture.

SETH CARNILL left London, and his career in the music industry, in 2009 and is now living in Amsterdam where he works as an interiors, lifestyle and wedding photographer for a variety of private and commercial clients. Seth often returns to the UK for work and, having grown up in Suffolk, has a profound love for the English countryside. Revisiting some of his favourite places while making this book made even navigating lockdowns and Covid tests worth it.

HOXTON MINI PRESS is a small indie publisher based in east London. We make books about London (and beyond) with a dedication to lovely production and personal stories. When we started the company, people told us 'print was dead'; we wanted to prove them wrong. Books are no longer about information but objects in their own right: things to collect and own and inspire.

First edition. Published in 2022 by Hoxton Mini Press, London.
Copyright © Hoxton Mini Press 2022. All rights reserved.

Text © Alex Bagner; photography © Seth Carnill; design by Matthew Young; copy-editing by Florence Filose; production by Anna De Pascale; production support by Becca Jones

ISBN: 978-1-914314-00-1

Printed and bound by OZGraf, Poland

Hoxton Mini Press is an environmentally conscious publisher, committed to offsetting our carbon footprint. The offset for this book was purchased from Stand For Trees. For every book you buy from our website, we plant a tree: www.hoxtonminipress.com

Contents

Florence and James uprooted their London flower business
and moved their young family to a farm in Cornwall (p.16).

Stuart and Polly are living out
their rural dream in Suffolk:
faithful hound and all (p.160).

Stuart and Polly's new home is a converted 17th-century barn
in the grounds of a ruined castle (p.160).

The sheer natural beauty of the Lake District counteracts
any London FOMO for Jeremy and Simon (p.84).

Swapping Dalston for the Cornish village of Penryn has let
young creatives Harry and El spend more time in the ocean (p.60).

Bayode and Claire's son Septimus makes the most of living in Margate, playing on the beach after school (p.28).

Since making a fresh start in Suffolk, Cathy has found new ways to keep busy; including volunteering at a woodland refuge (p.108).

Adolfo (*left*) and Craig (*right*) moved to the Kent coast so Adolfo could start a business with his best friend, James (p.230).

At Cat and Tobden's immersive nature retreat in Devon, their daughter Tanzen tells me she was 'born to be wild' (p.96).

Sally found leaving Hackney for Suffolk prompted a shift in her prorities (p.172).

Vishal and Jane's kids have a freedom to explore in Norfolk that just wasn't possible when the family lived in Leytonstone (p.72).

Surrounded by the scenery of his childhood in Devon, Hugo and his wife Olive have started a business (p.38).

Stuart and Polly have filled their new home in Suffolk with vintage objects that tell a story (p.160).

The small, creatively minded villages in Suffolk have been the perfect new stomping ground for artist Cathy (p.108).

James has found more time for the things that matter since moving to Cornwall (p.16).

Cat and Tobden now live in East Portlemouth on the south Devon coast (p.96).

Alex and her daughters, Maggie (*left*) and Celia (*centre*), with their dog Basil on Kingsdown Beach near their home.

So you're thinking of leaving?

I always thought I'd write a book. I never in a million years thought it would have this title.

For as long as I can remember, I've defined myself as urban. It's what I know, what I'm good at – it's in my core. I based my career as a magazine journalist around being able to navigate a city, seeking out the latest and the best. As a mother, I've staunchly opposed the idea that kids need open fields and chickens to be happy. Raising children in London creates smart, creative, open-minded, savvy and curious little minds. I was myself brought up in central London by culture-vulture parents whose idea of a relaxing family getaway was a city break to Paris. They were both originally from Stockholm so theirs was not necessarily a London-centric attitude, but for them it was quite simply a given that if you had the means, you would live as close to an urban centre as was possible.

But, in the summer of 2020, for the first time in my life, I bought myself a practical, fully waterproof jacket and started thinking, quite seriously, about leaving London.

Yep, I joined the troupe of Covid clichés out there whose views on what's possible, and what really matters, had suddenly been put in a spin. Since 'lockdown' first became a part of our lexicon, magazines and weekend supplements have been bursting with articles on the city exodus, the reappraisal of urban living, and the newfound flexibility offered by homeworking. Rural estate agents can't keep up with demand and urban city centres have been forced to reinvent themselves. There is something of the zeitgeist about this mass evacuation, certainly, but more than that there is a seismic shift happening in our thinking about city vs country life. The countryside has always had its own fresh, creative way of thinking, and it feels as though many city-dwellers are starting to crave this differing perspective on life.

My own story is a fairly standard of-the-moment tale. A holiday home, purchased ten years ago, offered me the opportunity to dip my toe into life by the sea: our cottage is on the shingle beach of Kingsdown, a village in Kent. As time went on we spent more time there, and when my husband left his job he bought a run-down pub called The Rose, on the high street of the nearby town of Deal. It started as a flutter but it quickly turned into a passion for both of us.

After major renovation, we re-opened The Rose as a restaurant, bar and hotel in May 2017. It's been a rollercoaster of a ride, not least because neither of us had any experience of working in hospitality. But we put our hearts and souls into the project and, with the help of lots of talented friends, created a place that people seem to have enjoyed coming to over the years.

The plan had always been to stay in London and run The Rose from a distance, but the travelling backwards and forwards started to take its toll. So, after much discussion, we decided to make our holiday town our home. My family and I have embarked on a new Just Left London chapter.

I'm fully aware of my advantaged position to be even contemplating a move, let alone having a place, and a community, so clearly marked out for me to jump to. But the truth is, when the idea of leaving London first came up I felt quite sick at the thought. What did it mean to leave the vibrant energy of the city for a new life by the coast? Would I be bored? Would I become boring? Would I ever move on from London FOMO?

As these (in hindsight, rather absurd) questions revolved around my mind, I began to realise I wasn't alone – either in starting to seriously consider leaving the capital, or in my wariness of doing so. Lots of people around me were also thinking and dreaming of what could possibly replace a well-spent London life. And many had the same questions and the same fears; the idea for this book began to form. So, I set out to meet some people who had already done it: families, couples and individuals spanning age, budget, background and circumstance but who all, for various reasons, had reinvented their lives outside of the city.

As I spoke to my interviewees, many of the most obvious reasons Londoners leave the city came up: a desire to simplify their lives, enjoy more space, get a dog. But behind these headlines, each person's motivations, desires and ways of making it work were unique, from a grandfather's ground-breaking project to build a sustainable home out of hemp in Cambridgeshire (p.220), to a young couple finding a way to adventure on a shoestring budget in Cornwall (p.60). I spoke to a family who prioritised building a community (p.148), and another who found

The restaurant at The Rose in Deal, which Alex now owns with her husband Christopher.

The Rose was a run-down pub when Alex and Christopher bought it in 2017; after a year of renovations, they transformed it into a vibrant hotel, bar and restaurant.

a sanctuary to spend time on their own (p.134). One married couple explained why they'd kept moving (p.84), while another showed me the wild garden where they hope to spend the rest of their lives (p.208).

As it's developed, I've found that – though not my original intention – this book has also become a celebration of the extraordinarily beautiful and eclectic English countryside. It's been a reminder of how lucky we are to live in a country that offers so many alternatives to London life, but is compact enough to mean the capital is never that far away. The stories I found grew organically and the geographical spread has been entirely random. In no way is this a complete tour of Britain, but it has been a privilege to be able to explore and admire this green and pleasant land from the Kent coast to the Cornish beaches, the Norfolk flats to the Cumbrian peaks. And though I'm not quite ready to rule out my own *How to Come Back* sequel yet, I hope that, through Seth Carnill's captivating images, you too will find inspiration in these pages if you're looking to re-lay your hat outside of the urban sprawl; you're just not sure where to set it yet.

Alex Bagner, 2022

How to move your business

Florence & James
Rejerrah, Cornwall

When this young family relocated to Cornwall,
they took their flower delivery start-up with them
– now, business is blooming

Some people seem programmed to live in cities; some flourish in the wilds of the countryside; and some, you get the feeling, would thrive anywhere. Husband and wife James and Florence Kennedy are the latter kind of couple – fearless, adventurous, and utterly inspirational in their sense of fun and their lack of limits when it comes to what's possible. But while they were both confident they'd cultivate a happy home for their young family wherever they ended up, what took them by surprise when they left London in early 2020 was the phenomenal effect a life outside the capital had on their flower business.

In London, Florence and James were the poster kids for urban living. They'd converted a unique former dairy, tucked between terraced houses in Clapton, Hackney, into a live/work space where they hosted events and photoshoots. James also manufactured bespoke bicycles and Florence, meanwhile, launched Petalon: an online florist's that started out

James and Florence wanted a 'project';
renovating a dilapidated cottage into a
beautiful family home in less than a year
certainly provided them with one.

*'We loved city life, but if
it wasn't going to be London,
we wanted something
completely different.'*

delivering beautiful, affordable bouquets by bike across the city.

When the lease on their London home came to an end, their options to buy a similar size place and stay within their area were severely restricted by finances. 'I would have gladly stayed in Clapton, maybe even forever,' says James, 'but there was just nothing in our budget for us there.' Having made the decision not to move to the suburbs or try another city, they started to get excited about building a life in the countryside: 'If it wasn't going to be London, we wanted something completely different.'

The couple, who are both originally from Bath, were open to all options – as long as they met three criteria: it had to fit their budget, they wanted space and land to spread out and potentially keep animals, and they decided they were looking for something 'derelict' that would provide a project. So, when a sprawling, dilapidated farmhouse in inland Cornwall came up – 'for the same price as a two-bedroom, ex-council flat in Clapton' – they jumped on it. They moved in May 2020, in the middle of the first lockdown, and in less than a year turned the bedraggled cottage into a spacious, stylish home. Having relocated Petalon, they began growing a flower farm from scratch – cultivating unique British field flowers, which they now sell alongside their array of seasonal bouquets – and demand has just kept growing.

'James has gone into complete overdrive since we moved,' Florence tells me as she takes me on a tour of their flower-filled fields. It's a Tuesday afternoon in late May, the sun is shining and the farm is a hive of activity. In the barn, the floristry team chat cheerfully while creating vibrant bouquets, ready to be shipped off in eco-packaging across the country. Outside, where Florence experiments with new and unusual blooms across 40 flowerbeds and two huge polytunnels, we find James busy shovelling earth and watering the beds. 'I mean, he's never been a sit-on-the-sofa-all-day-with-his-phone kinda guy,' says Florence. 'But since we got here, the amount of DIY projects he manages to achieve every day has become ridiculous.' James laughs, agreeing: 'Boredom is not

something I've struggled with during lockdown. I love how, here, I'm completely awake in the day and then so tired at night.'

I am blown away by how much they have done in such a short amount of time. Did they always have this kind of set-up in mind? 'Oh my goodness, no,' replies Florence. 'Cornwall, the flower farm – none of this was planned. To begin with it was just about moving our family [the couple have two children: Clover, four, and Oshi, 18 months]; we thought Petalon would remain in London and we'd run it from afar. But then slowly things fell into place. We found this house that came with all this land and thought it'd be fun to give growing the flowers a go, rather than just importing them. Then we came across a lovely flower farmer called Claire who lives in the next-door village who showed us the ropes. The rest has just been a series of trials, tutorials and errors.' She has an incisive yet relaxed manner, which, combined with James's insatiable can-do attitude, is clearly what fuels this business.

It's also what fuels them as a family; James completely remodelled the cottage they now live in with only the help of his father. It's now an elegantly crafted home, surrounded by a healthy vegetable patch and a noisy chicken coop that add to the hard-working, good-life vibe. As Florence drives off to get the kids from nursery, James starts to prepare supper for their return – pasta sauce made from a variety of homegrown tomatoes – and I ask if he finds it hard to demark time for the family now they essentially live within their workplace. 'Work and play have become a little bit more intertwined here, it's true,' James replies. 'But our business has always evolved around the family. We both take every Wednesday off and the weekends are strictly about the kids. Plus, we make time to enjoy where we are. It's so beautiful here for walks and swimming in the river.'

So does he miss London at all? 'I think Florence and I are both the same in that we've been very happy in every one of our homes, but when we move on, we move on. We're not sentimental about places or stuff around us, and we don't look back.'

The barn opposite the couple's home
has been transformed into a workspace
where all of the Petalon bouquets are
made then shipped off in eco-packaging
across the country.

'Boredom is not something I've struggled with during lockdown. I love how, here, I'm completely awake in the day and then so tired at night.'

James wanted to 'buy new' as little as
possible for their home, preferring to source
furniture that had a few stories to tell.

The couple have created two polytunnels and 40 rows of flowerbeds, so they can now offer bouquets cut straight from their farm.

BEST ADVICE WE WERE GIVEN

'Everything is a system of trial and error. If you don't give things a go, and make mistakes, you'll never learn.'

ADVICE WE'D GIVE

'Commit to where you are. Keep all the fond memories of London, but look ahead and move on.'

How to keep your identity

Bayode & Claire
Margate, Kent

Nearly a decade after they swapped skyscrapers for sandcastles, this husband and wife feel leaving the capital hasn't changed who they are

Are we defined by where we live? No doubt a sense of place helps to creating a feeling of belonging, but for Bayode and Claire Oduwole – who moved from Queen's Park to Margate in 2014 – how they identify themselves is based on far more than their decision to leave the city. This husband and wife duo, who are co-founders of the fashion and bespoke tailoring business Pokit, are determined to stay true to who they are and where they've come from.

Neither of them had ever been to Margate before when they first stumbled upon the Georgian terraced house where they now live, minutes from the seafront. 'The rent on our shop in Soho was up and we couldn't afford to renew it,' Claire recalls. 'We were initially looking in Bath for an un-modernised Georgian house that we could renovate into a live/work space. A friend mentioned you could get beautiful, big houses in Margate; we saw this house

Bayode, Claire and their son Septimus live
a five-minute walk from Margate Beach.

'There are all sorts of people here, it's eclectic and random, and we thrive off that.'

online and came over to see it. We knew as soon as we walked through the door that this was the one. It was January and the weather was awful, but we had a wander down to the seafront, had a bag of chips, then went back, called the agent and bought it.'

Despite thinking she'd made a terrible mistake on the first night they moved in – 'the seagulls were so loud I couldn't sleep,' she laughs – Claire, Bayode and their 8-year-old son Septimus soon found themselves adapting to a life of space and sea air. Claire and Bayode began stripping back the house, revealing the grand residence it had once been. 'We haven't put anything in, just taken back,' Bayode explains of their playful sanctuary, from which they now run Pokit as an online business. Rather than knocking down walls and repainting everything they could put a brush to, they've kept the original wallpaper and given each of the many rooms a function, be it the 'gallery', the 'hat room' or the 'music room'. With not a glimpse of mid-century in sight, this house has a refreshing lack of clichés.

Which is exactly how Bayode and Claire intended it. Their aesthetic is so genuinely unique, and their way of life so entirely their own, that it's hard to define in words, let alone attach it to a place. 'We do still have a healthy dose of west London scepticism,' Bayode says, laughing, 'which is why we're able to stand back and take this new DFL ["Down from London"] enthusiasm that is trickling in with a pinch of salt.' They have seen Margate evolve in the seven years they've lived there and are very aware of the huge shift that has taken place recently. 'When we first moved here, only a few young families had come from London. It's different now; the freelancers and people working from home are moving in from the east London creative scene. They're young, entrepreneurial, energetic and obsessed with forming a community of like-minded people.'

While Bayode and Claire have mixed feelings around this 'Hackney-fication', they can't help but be happy about the influx of new cafés, restaurants and shops that have sprung up (and are even wondering if the time is now right to open their own retail space here). They believe movement of people is beneficial for all layers of society – not just those moving. But there's still no dominant 'type' of person in the town, they tell me – and it's this openness and welcoming nature that they love: 'There are all sorts of people here, it's eclectic and random, and we thrive off that. The diversity – and by that I mean difference, not necessarily ethnicity – is wonderful. In London that doesn't happen; you exist in tribes and everyone is the same and together,' says Bayode. 'This fixation that London is the only place that is open-minded and liberal comes with its own conceit,' he continues. 'When we moved here, I thought I'd have to drive to Peckham to get my Nigerian grocery fix but turns out there's an African supermarket down the road. I was the one who was prejudiced.'

So have they really not changed at all since leaving London? 'I think our lives were changing anyway with having a family. But leaving places does affect people. Of course it does,' says Claire. 'But,' adds Bayode, 'if you are gregarious, you can live anywhere. If you are strong enough and detached enough you can live anywhere. I think to have less of a sense of identity tied to space is what makes you strong.' And I have no doubt that Bayode and Claire's ability to maintain their wonderfully unique lifestyle is down to their strength of character. I ask if they miss the city, all the same. 'London was good to me,' replies Bayode. 'I had a really great time there. But what Dr Johnson said about being tired of London is nonsense – truth is, you just move on.'

'This fixation that London is the only place that is open-minded and liberal comes with its own conceit.'

The couple have turned the whole
ground floor of their home into a gallery
space to display their ever-evolving
collection of art and furniture.

Wanting to preserve the history of their new home, Claire and Bayode stripped back the walls of the sitting room to reveal its original wallpaper.

'If you are gregarious, you can live anywhere.'

The couple now run their bespoke tailoring
business, Pokit, from a light-filled room at the
back of the house, while upstairs even Septimus
has his own workspace.

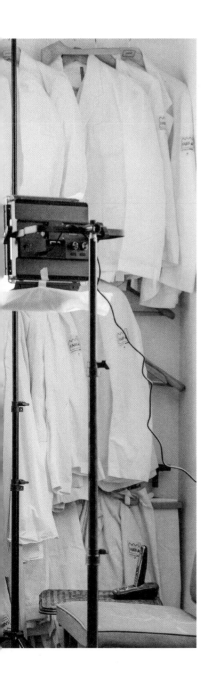

BEST ADVICE WE WERE GIVEN

'We spoke to a friend who had lived in the same house for 50 years; she said she found it hard to define different phases of her life and advised us to keep moving every so often. Change is good.'

ADVICE WE'D GIVE

'Don't be too specific in where and what you move to, be open to new adventures as they arise. And if you want a beautiful big house, forget about being cosy. Being warm is something you are when you go to visit friends, who live in flats, in London.'

How to move back home

Hugo & Olive
Colyton, Devon

When this entrepreneurial couple bought the house
that one of them grew up in, they found returning
home actually meant taking a big leap forwards

For husband and wife Hugo and Olive Guest, the
hunt for a home to raise a family in took them far
and wide; across Italy, to London, and finally –
back to the place where Hugo grew up. In 2018,
the couple left Brixton and secured funding to buy
Hugo's former family home, deep in the Devonshire
countryside, and turn it into a boutique hotel and
farm-to-table restaurant.

'It does feel a bit like history is repeating itself,'
says Hugo. 'I see my son, Rufus, now a year old,
pushing his toy tractor on the lawn, and nothing has
changed from photos of me doing the same thing
35 years ago. The woods, the fields, the view; it's all
the same.'

Despite this déjà vu, in many ways the couple's
new life couldn't be more different to what they're

'*Our business plan was always based around doing
it here, in this house, in this unique location.*'

used to. 'I was working in advertising in Soho, Hugo was working in insurance in the City,' Olive tells me. 'Until early 2020, we lived the full London life.' But, after eight years of the capital's grindstone, both Hugo and Olive were starting to feel restless with their careers. Olive, who grew up in Suffolk, practices as a landscape painter, and found herself craving nature for inspiration; Hugo was keen to pursue his passion for food. So when his parents – who had run a B&B from Glebe House, their former Georgian vicarage, for 15 years – announced they were looking to retire, Hugo had an idea.

'It didn't exactly happen overnight, but from the first moment we discussed it, the idea just wouldn't go away,' reflects Hugo. He and Olive spent years planning around the kitchen table, researching and applying to grants until, finally, the dream started to take shape. In 2017, Hugo quit his City job and enrolled in the Ashburton Cookery School. He honed his skills as a chef in well-regarded London restaurants including The Marksman in Hackney and Robin Gill's Sorella in Clapham, then took himself off to Tuscany to learn all he could about traditional pig farming, Italian food and *agriturismi*: independent family-run farms with rooms and restaurants that serve homemade, locally sourced food. In early 2020, he, Olive, and their three-month-old son, Rufus, packed up their flat and moved back to east Devon to turn his parents' home into an English *agriturismo*, inspired by this Italian tradition.

Olive set to work on an extensive renovation of the house, collaborating with an interior designer friend to source antiques, choose paint colours and hang the walls with art: a mix of local artists, eBay finds and her own work. Hugo meanwhile had his sights set on turning the garage into a bakery and temperature-controlled ageing room for his salami

and pickles, installing a polytunnel in the garden and a pig farm in the 16-acre grounds. Hugo's parents have now moved out of the main house into a converted outbuilding, while they look to buy their own home close by.

'Things were a little tense at first,' Olive admits, recalling the initial period of time when they lived together with Hugo's parents in the main house, and the renovation took place around them. 'We all had to tread very carefully. They had to try and not interfere even when they thought my ideas were ridiculous... And I had to respect their opinions. But they gave us both space and ultimately were excited for us. Today they are very much part of the house and they often come out and greet guests – but it is our business now, and our home.'

Certainly, the couple have made Glebe House their own. From Olive's creative interiors to Hugo's determination to bake, cook and farm everything on site, the guesthouse is spilling over with their warm, welcoming touches. 'We are determined to make everything ourselves,' they tell me proudly. Since opening in spring 2021, the couple have moved out into a small cabin in the grounds, leaving the main house just for guests. I ask if it's not a little odd having people they don't know in their home the whole time; 'The place is small with only five rooms and 30 covers in the restaurant, so it never feels impersonal,' replies Olive. Hugo, on the other hand, tells me he got used to welcoming in strangers long ago; he was 16 when his parents first began their B&B.

But could they have made their dream work somewhere they weren't so connected to? 'No, never,' insists Hugo. 'This plan was always based around doing it here, in this house, in this unique location. It's a celebration of where we are and that's the joy of it.'

'I see my son Rufus pushing his toy tractor on the lawn, and nothing has changed from photos of me doing the same thing 35 years ago.'

'We are determined to make everything ourselves.'

Hugo has turned the garage into a temperature-controlled ageing room for his homemade salami and pickles.

'The guesthouse is small with only
five rooms and 30 covers in the restaurant,
so it never feels impersonal.'

Olive worked with an interior designer friend
to choose wallpapers, source antiques and hang
the walls of Glebe House with art.

The food Hugo serves his guests is joyfully simple: everything has been prepared by hand with obvious care and enthusiasm.

BEST ADVICE WE WERE GIVEN

'My parents ran the B&B all by themselves, but my mum always advised me to get help where I could. We've been so lucky; we've managed to find an amazing team of people to work with us, and to learn from.'

ADVICE WE'D GIVE

'If you have an idea, however crazy, but you believe in it, don't let it slip. Where there's a will to do something, there is always a way.'

How to not be afraid of change

Andrew Downs
Deal, Kent

Andrew never planned to leave the capital,
but caring for his mum Sheila has meant
embracing a new life by the sea

For some, leaving London is a lifelong dream; for others, it's more of a spontaneous move. For Andrew Downs, it was neither. When I ask why he made the move from London to Deal, he's very clear: 'Being here is not how I intended it, but it's part of my life journey.'

Andrew has always been one to embrace change and confesses to being a 'little addicted' to renovating houses. From a Shoreditch warehouse to a Chelsea mews, to a west London penthouse, the 'life journey' he speaks of has so far seen him and his husband Jeff move between 21 different houses in the last 35 years: across London as well as New York, Moscow and the French countryside. Andrew and Jeff together ran James English Productions, a photo production agency specialising in large fashion shoots, and for the last two decades have enjoyed a lifestyle split between weekdays immersed in the

When lockdown
started, Andrew
moved out of
London so he
could care for his
mum, Sheila.

energy of the city, and weekends spent entertaining in their seaside townhouse in the heart of Deal's conservation area.

But then Covid hit. With no large-scale shoots able to go ahead and budgets pulled, their business was suddenly put on hold. Andrew meanwhile was worried about his mother, Sheila, who was living on her own in Sandwich. He invited her to come and live with them in Deal, where the couple had decided to see out the first lockdown. After a few months, two things became clear: keeping their London home was hard to justify financially, and returning home had become an impossibility for Sheila.

'She has stroke-related vascular dementia, so she can't live on her own, but she's not ready to go into a home. I knew that she had to come live with us, there was just no other option.' This meant having to leave their beloved Deal house and instead buy a Victorian terraced townhouse, which had a flat beneath it for Sheila. 'I want her to feel like she is independent, with her own front door and patio, even if I'm here to give her constant support,' Andrew explains.

'We sold up and bought this place in August 2020,' Andrew tells me. 'It hadn't been touched since the 70s, so I set to work replacing absolutely everything. It wasn't the easiest stint of my life, living with Mum in a small Airbnb while we renovated this place, but it has given me a new relationship with her, made me a more patient human and I certainly appreciate what a wonderful husband I have.' He is showing me around their new townhouse, which is filled with Andrew's eclectic collection of art and royal memorabilia.

From the antique wallpaper to the ornate drawing room, where the colour scheme is based on a ballroom in Kensington that Andrew spotted in an issue of *The Savoy* magazine from 1895, Andrew's interiors are as sumptuous as they are flamboyant. 'Mind you, I always want to do a raw Georgian thing with an oak table and one single brass candlestick,' he laughs, 'but every time I end up back in the opulent 1890s.'

As well as completely reinventing the house's story, Andrew's experience of caring for his mum has also inspired him to reinvent his business. His latest venture, Edited Photos, designs elegant memory boxes to help trigger thoughts and recollections in people suffering from memory loss. 'I'm working with a good friend who lives up the road and the idea is to start selling the project to care homes across the country.' It may be a million miles away from his previous jet-setting career, but it's hugely rewarding. 'My life is certainly very different now. In many ways I wasn't ready to give up my London life when I did – I loved it, and at 55 I feel far too young to be here, but this is where I need to be right now. Keeping my head above water and looking after my mum.'

'So, 55 is too young to move to Deal?' I ask hesitantly (after all, I've recently moved here myself). 'Well, you can always move back,' he laughs. 'We have some friends in their early 30s who have just left Stoke Newington and bought a house here. I think they're mad. Lockdown, Brexit these are mere blips for London. It's been through much worse and bounced back with force. But they can always move back, and now at least they're on the property ladder.'

Will he and Jeff be heading back to London when circumstances change? 'We're definitely leaving this house for something less tall and thin as soon as that's an option, but no, I think we're in Deal now. We have an amazing network that keeps us here. We're always entertaining and going to other people's houses, which I love. I think, in London, people stopped asking us round about 10 or 15 years ago,' Andrew chuckles. I ask if that means he feels he's chosen to live here now; 'No,' he replies, 'I feel like I've washed up here, but that's okay. There are worse places to wash up. It can't be everyone's journey to look after their parents, I realise that – it's just not possible for everyone – but it's my journey, and I'm making the most of it.'

'I feel like I've washed up here,
but that's okay. There are worse
places to wash up.'

Andrew was inspired by the opulent 1890s when choosing
the sumptuous colour palette of their home.

Having Sheila move in downstairs has meant Andrew can be there for his mum, but she can still live independently.

BEST ADVICE I WAS GIVEN

'Don't fall out with anyone; it's not worth it in a small town. Always smile.'

ADVICE I'D GIVE

'Do a cooking course. Outside of London you have to learn how to entertain and have people over. It's ungracious to accept invitations from everyone and never invite anyone back.'

59

How to work from anywhere

Harry & El
Penryn, Cornwall

Why stop at working from home? This young, creative couple have found an innovative way to take their desks on the road

If the Covid pandemic has made one thing clear, it's that work is not tied to a place or a time. The sudden explosion of homeworking released many people who had already left the city from relentless commutes; but it also opened up the possibility for many, many more workers to give living outside of London a go.

I saw plenty of enviable home offices while compiling this book, from converted outbuildings surrounded by nature to book-lined studios. But when it came to perfecting the art of remote working, none had it quite so nailed as Harry Ingrams and El McQuaid. In search of a way to work productively, while also being able to spend their lunchbreaks surfing, Harry and El came up with an ingenious twist on the home office set-up: a desk that travels with you.

When the pandemic hit, Harry, a graphic designer, and El, who works for a construction

The mobile-office-in-a-van the couple have created
allows them to take their work all the way to the beach.

'We wanted to live full lives outside of work;
to enjoy the coast while we're here.'

company, escaped the confines of their cramped flatshare in Dalston for the village of Penryn in west Cornwall. But, though they both craved a bit more space and sea air, this was not a quest to take it easy – at least not where their careers were concerned. Harry's freelance work was picking up fast and El combines a busy work schedule with studying for a Master's degree in Architecture. 'We keep a strict working day,' Harry explains. 'We're very much still on London hours, working 8am till 6pm, and sometimes even longer. But we still wanted to live full lives outside of work, too – to enjoy the coast while we're here. So we came up with the mobile-office-in-a-van idea...'

The van, a former Welsh police dog unit vehicle that the couple picked up in Reading for £5,000, is quite the invention. A large solar panel on the roof charges a battery pack to which you can plug in phones and laptops. The back is entirely sound-proofed and carpeted should you need to take a call, and the interior has been given a complete plywood overhaul. Overseen by Harry's father, a Design and Technology teacher, Harry and El have added two pull-out desks, a few shelves and drawers and a bench seat, plus plenty of tucked-away storage spaces – handy for stashing wetsuits for a sunset dip in the sea. 'It's not a place to work full-time or anything,' says Harry. 'But it just means we can prolong the time we're away from our desks and be a bit more flexible.'

In many ways, they've hit the jackpot in life; yet it does seem something of a slower pace for this young, active couple – who met in London and only moved in together as lockdown hit. While their work-life balance is inspiring, I wonder if, as ambitious early-career creatives, they feel like they are missing out on opportunities to grow their networks. 'I guess meeting people is a bit more limited here,' says Harry. 'But I think that's a positive as well as a negative. With constant exposure to excitement, I find you're always chasing the next thing, which is exhausting and not productive. In London it was all about making plans for tomorrow and what you're doing next. I'm living in the present and happy to be here.' And, though Penryn is tiny, it has a growing community of like-minded creatives – either attracted, like Harry and El, by the possibility of working remotely from one of England's most beautiful counties, or else setting up their own businesses in the village.

So will the couple stay in Cornwall, or will their cleverly adapted van inspire them to keep moving? 'We've been thinking of maybe travelling a bit in Ireland or Scotland. But we're not nomads or surfer-travellers like that. The van extends our lifestyle but we like having beds and hot showers,' El laughs. 'Plus,' adds Harry, 'there may well be a time for us to go back to London. It will always be there, and that feels very reassuring.'

Harry is a keen fisherman and makes the most
of living so close to the Cornish coast.

'In London it was all about making plans for tomorrow and what you're doing next. Here, I'm living in the present.'

'We're not nomads or surfer-travellers like that. The van extends our lifestyle but we like having beds and hot showers.'

El had never surfed before the couple moved to Penryn. Now, she regularly spends her evenings in the ocean.

'There may well come a time for us to
move back. London will always be there,
and that feels very reassuring.'

BEST ADVICE WE WERE GIVEN

'I remember a friend telling us not to take leaving London lightly. Don't underestimate how much you're leaving behind and how much work it is to build up good, new friends.'

ADVICE WE'D GIVE

'Make sure you have some kind of purpose when you leave, something to give you structure and shape your week. Don't be surprised if you're left twiddling your thumbs a bit as you settle into a new pace of life.'

How to slow down

Jane & Vishal
Wells-next-the-Sea, Norfolk

When these two London creatives moved out to
a fisherman's cottage by the sea, they found new,
more sustainable ways to feel inspired

'I wanted to move to a place where I could always see
the horizon,' explains Jane Money, beaming, as we
walk across magnificent Holkham beach near her
home in Norfolk. 'I thought, if we're going to leave
London, we might as well go somewhere utterly
stunning.' And so, in October 2019, when her boss
refused her request to work part of the week from
home, Jane quit her job as Head of Creative at a large
fashion company so she, her husband Vishal and

their two children, 11-year-old Ziggi and eight-year-
old Daisy-Mae, could swap their terraced house in
Leytonstone for a cottage on the Norfolk coast.

'It's ironic really how things have turned out,'
she muses, as we meet in late spring 2021. 'Today the
office is basically shut with the entire 400-strong
team working from home.' Jane now works freelance
as a marketing and brand consultant, from an office
that is actually a summer house which Vishal built

The family take the short walk from their house
to their allotment together most days.

Vishal has started
a food delivery
business, The Jolly
Indian Sailor,
using vegetables
grown on the
family's allotment.

on their allotment using mostly found and foraged materials. We visit it later that day; a verdant field under the big Norfolk sky, divided into plots: each lovingly tended to by a different one of their neighbours. 'I download documents or hotspot off my phone, and it's just a wonderful place to read and think and be creative,' Jane says of her unusual office space. 'My work requires me to have ideas so it's much harder to be tied to a dull desk every day. Here, I can take little inspirational breaks and go water some plants or weed a bed. And then, just as my laptop battery is running out, it's time to pop off and get the kids from school.'

Vishal, a former retail designer whose past clients include Dover Street Market and Levi's, is today equally inspired by their allotment. He has just started a new business, The Jolly Indian Sailor, a weekly food door-drop service, made for the most part using ingredients grown by him and Jane. 'Food and cooking has always been a personal passion, but turning that into a business in London just felt relentless. Here I can do it my way, from the heart, like I was taught to cook by my mum,' says Vishal as he spoons out his homemade *sambharo* (a chilli, carrot, cabbage and pepper salad) and *bataka pauwa* (flattened rice with peanuts, potatoes and fresh green chutney) for us to try.

After we've eaten, Jane and Daisy-Mae give me a tour of the herb garden, their various tomato plants and the root vegetable patch, proudly pointing out what's growing. It's clear that the family derives an enormous feeling of accomplishment from this small patch of land. 'I'm quite obsessed by it,' Jane confesses. 'I just love the trial and tribulation of planting and seeing what works and what doesn't. It makes me feel very settled and happy.' They are about to take on a second allotment, which will mean they can grow more than enough to sustain themselves and Vishal's food business. 'Becoming self-sufficient wasn't necessarily our end goal, but taking the time to understand the cycle of the seasons is such a lovely thing. We've also got into pickling and preserving vegetables for when there are gluts in the growing.'

It's just under two years since Jane and Vishal moved here, but the couple had been plotting their escape from London for some time. 'I was leaving home at 7.45am and not getting back till 7.45pm at night,' says Jane. 'Squashing into the underground every day of the week. I remember thinking, this can't be the only way to live.' But as Vishal points out, had they not lived in London where they could tire of a commute, they would never have ended up where they are now: 'It's all part of the journey.' And was their specific spot in the small town of Wells-next-the-Sea always going to be part of that journey? 'For sure,' replies Vishal. 'We used to come to Norfolk looking for vintage furniture, and then for holidays with the children. We have always loved coming to this part of the world – it's such a special place. But houses here just don't come up. We were looking for four years before we found this one and pounced on it.'

It's not hard to see the appeal of the place; their cottage is steps away from Wells' serene harbour, where fish-and-chip shops overlook boats bringing in the daily catch. I ask Vishal if it was hard settling in to live in a place that is also a holiday destination, and a haven for second homes. 'We are surrounded by holiday lets but that doesn't bother us so much,' he says. 'If anything it makes us feel lucky to live here, we don't need to pack up on a Sunday evening. But it did take longer than we thought to settle in. Especially at the school; there were quite a few "you're not from round 'ere" looks at first. But now we laugh with the other parents about it.'

So do they miss anything about London life? 'We miss our friends and our house, for sure. But no, even that question feels very "London",' says Jane. 'I have a different mindset here. I go for walks and sit down and do nothing; I never used to do that. I've slowed down and I feel healthier and happier and, as I kept telling my old boss, I'm pretty sure I get more done. But then, I think – I hope – she's figured that one out for herself by now!'

'Squashing into the underground every day,
I remember thinking, this can't be the only way to live.'

The couple's two children, Ziggi and Daisy-Mae, have a new freedom to explore that just wasn't possible in London.

BEST ADVICE WE WERE GIVEN

'A friend who made the countryside leap before us said it's important to not think leaving London is going to instantly solve everything. Our son still plays Fortnite a bit more than we'd ideally like, but at least here it's a nice balance between that and going out kayaking.'

ADVICE WE'D GIVE

'Don't rush buying. We took our time to find a place in the exact spot we wanted and we're so pleased we didn't cave in earlier, so we didn't end up somewhere further inland or away from the town.'

83

How to not slow down at all

Jeremy & Simon
Underbarrow, Cumbria

Who says people move to the countryside to take it easy? For this dynamic and ambitious couple, it's simply been a chance to set new goals

'I'm not very good at doing nothing,' Jeremy Langmead (*pictured left*) confesses as he shows me around the immaculate farmhouse in Cumbria that he owns with his husband, Simon Rayner. It's a weekday in mid-May when I visit this 'land of lakes, mountains and Wordsworth', as Jeremy refers to his surroundings. The house, which is cottagecore through and through, is utterly tranquil – chickens roam on the drive, horses graze in the field beyond

and the far-reaching views are breathtaking. It may well be, as Wordsworth believed, 'the loveliest spot that man hath found', but it's still slightly baffling to find this media power couple in the small rural village of Underbarrow. For Jeremy is ex-editor-in-chief of *Wallpaper** magazine, *Esquire* and *Mr Porter*, while Simon founded the innovative marketing start-up 'PR in a Box'. So how did they get here?

'Well, I do love a view,' Jeremy says, grinning,

Jeremy and Simon's new home is surrounded by
the beauty of the Lake District National Park.

'When you say you're in the Lake District, no one tries to convince you to go to a press launch.'

as we head inside. But as we cradle cups of tea around the AGA (of course), he expands on their decision to leave the city. 'I think it's perhaps to do with getting beyond the London FOMO barrier,' he says. 'I love going out but I'm terrible at saying no. Here, I'm safe – it would take me four hours to get to The Lansdowne [his local in Primrose Hill] – they'd all have gone home by the time I got there.' Simon laughs and adds, 'When you say you're in the Lake District, no one tries to convince you to go to a press launch.' While one shouldn't underestimate the power of London FOMO (or the persuasion tactics of a good PR), perhaps even more significant in their decision was the fact that where they are now is too far away from London to commute on a daily, or even weekly, basis.

In fact, Jeremy and Simon have already moved house twice since leaving the capital, and each time they've found themselves moving steadily further away from it – first Hertfordshire, then Suffolk, now Cumbria, where they arrived just as the first lockdown hit in March 2020. Was the plan always to keep relocating? 'Not at all,' says Jeremy. 'We threw ourselves into each home, creating a new personality for each space – and a new way of life.' But for various reasons – 'in a nutshell: Hertfordshire was far too big and in Suffolk, we didn't love our location' – they decided to keep their journey going.

As a result, they both left their full-time jobs in 2020, and now divide their time between various freelance ventures. Jeremy writes a fashion column

for *The Times*, has just authored a book about the new frontiers of male grooming, *Vain Glorious*, and is launching a men's skincare brand. Simon has sold his PR company, and is working with a friend to renovate and reopen a local inn, while working flat-out at the pub down the road to learn the ropes. Combined with a side project of running a bunch of holiday lets, it's safe to say that for all Jeremy and Simon's talk of 'watching *Baywatch* and taking up cross-stitching on the sofa', neither are quite ready to reduce their pace.

Still, Jeremy assures me, it's a far cry from their heady London days of going out after work *every* night. 'These days, I get my kicks from climbing mountains and watching the rhododendrons grow in the drive. They grow extraordinarily well here in the Lake District, something to do with the soil.' Meanwhile, Simon has fully embraced his new rural lifestyle: riding horses, building dry-stone walls and regularly checking – 'and thanking, oddly' – the robot lawnmower.

But what's most admirable, and indeed enviable, about Jeremy and Simon is their pervading 'why not?' approach. They begin each new project with insatiable energy, yet happily admit when things aren't quite right and it's time to move on. Will that be the case with their Cumbrian cottage, now that Covid restrictions are easing and the gravitational pull of the capital increasing? 'No,' asserts Jeremy. 'I think we're here for a while now, I feel settled here.' A beat later, he adds: 'But I do still look at Rightmove every day – just to see what's out there.'

The couple have already moved twice
since leaving London, and each of
their new homes has meant a complete
redecoration (though some pieces, like
their huge, beloved oil paintings, have
travelled with them).

'We've thrown ourselves into each new home, creating a personality for each space.'

Jeremy's new home office looks out over
the Cumbrian landscape; quite a contrast
to his London workplace that had views
of a dual carriageway.

'I'm not very good at doing nothing.'

'*These days, I get my kicks from climbing mountains and watching the rhododendrons grow in the drive.*'

BEST ADVICE WE WERE GIVEN

'I'm not sure it's advice so much as a warning, but I remember a friend telling us there are good houseguests and bad ones, and until you move out of London and have people to stay, you have no idea which friends will fall into which camp.'

ADVICE WE'D GIVE

'There's never a good time for anything, you've just got to jump on things when they come up. Make mistakes and then make them better. Oh, and robot lawnmowers really are amazing.'

How to
never look back

Cat & Tobden
East Portlemouth, Devon

Cat's friends said she'd be back in a month;
ten years later, she and her family have created
a whole new business and lifestyle

'I was born to be wild, that's my purpose,' says Tanzen, Cat Middleditch and Tobden Bodh's five-year-old daughter, in response to my question, 'What do you want to be when you grow up?' Tanzen is showing me around one of six polytunnels at her parents' five-acre small holding on the south Devon coast. This one is filled with all sorts of edible and non-edible plants, including strawberries and mulberries, which she offers to me as she tells me the names of many other salads, herbs and fruits I have never heard of.

Among the growing greenery in the polytunnel, there are a few armchairs dotted around as well as a coffee table, a guitar, some bongos and a table full of kids' craft materials. And there are people wandering through it chatting as they pick salad leaves, while in the next-door field, a yoga class is about to start. What all this amounts to is the High Nature

Cat grows a huge variety of edible and non-edible plants at her wilderness retreat, the High Nature Centre.

Centre: an ever-evolving, ecologically and socially inclusive hub dedicated to connecting with nature, growing food and promoting wellbeing, rewilding, social outreach and regenerative culture. Tanzen and I walk over to Cat, founder, creative director and permaculture designer of High Nature, who is busy checking in some guests for a Wild Running retreat. I instantly get the feeling that she too may be 'born to be wild'.

'Did she really say that? That's so funny!' exclaims Cat with a beaming grin. 'Wild' may not be the official term she uses, but when it comes to living and working in a harmonious way with nature, Cat certainly shares a purpose with her daughter. She set up the High Nature project in 2009, and today it hosts all sorts of events and retreats in the tunnels, has a small yurt camp to host guests and an al fresco 'dig and dine' restaurant. They have also just been granted permission to build a low-impact permanent roundhouse, designs for which are based on an iron age Celtic structure, where she, her husband Tobden (who she met in Goa six years ago) and Tanzen will base themselves in the summer months.

Though, unlike Tanzen, Cat wasn't actually 'born' into this lifestyle at all. Her parents, she admits, may have been a little bohemian in their ways – 'we were all brought up vegetarian and there was lots of camping' – but she was raised in the London suburb of Kingston upon Thames, went to university in Brighton and later settled in London where she worked as a graphic designer. It was there that she first enrolled in a permaculture course and became fascinated by the philosophy of working with, rather than against, nature. She soon realised that, while she loved London, her cramped and overpopulated surroundings just didn't feel right and the call of the wild beckoned.

'My London friends gave me a month and said I'd be back in no time. They thought I was too much of a people person and I'd get bored in the country-side without gigs and clubs to go to,' Cat recalls. Undeterred, she quit her job, went freelance, moved into her then-boyfriend's caravan in Totnes, and planned to spend her time 'growing plants and vegetables, building a house and living like a hobbit.' As it happened, planning restraints put a stop to them building their own 'hobbit house'; but Cat meanwhile had met a couple who let her use their fields and polytunnel to grow fruit and vegetables. In a stroke of serendipity, Cat inherited some money from her grandmother around the same time her friends decided to sell the land, and in 2009 she became the proud owner of this five-acre plot.

Acquiring the land may have felt like fate, but turning it from a run-down market garden to the community hub and enterprise it is today didn't just happen overnight. It has been a rural rollercoaster that, 12 years in, is still very much evolving. Along with multiple social outreach projects, hosting volunteer farmers (or 'WWOOFers' – through Worldwide Opportunities on Organic Farms) and regular community events, the new hospitality aspect of the business continues to grow.

Factor in that Cat and Tobden usually spend their winters in Goa, where until recently Cat also ran a café, along with their determined intentions to home-school Tanzen, and you get some sense of the dynamic lifestyle the family have chosen. 'We refuse to let ourselves be tied down by conventional systems,' Cat tells me. In many ways, perhaps the gregarious nature of a big city *would* have been more suited to her unconventional way of living. However, it's her passion for existing in harmony with nature that not only gives her new ideas and fresh conviction every day, but has also, she admits, come to define who she is and what she stands for. 'Nothing's forever,' she tells me in response to my question as to whether there's a timeframe for the project. 'We're making it up as we go along a bit, but being here and living this way is our purpose, for sure.'

Cat and Tobden have turned one of
the fields at their smallholding into
a yurt camp to attract holiday makers.

*'We refuse to let ourselves
be tied down by conventional
systems.'*

Tobden, Cat and
their daughter
Tanzen picking
salad leaves in the
polytunnel.

'We're making it up as we go along a bit,
but being here and living this way
is our purpose, for sure.'

'My London friends said I'd get bored in the countryside without gigs and clubs to go to.'

At the High Nature Centre on the south Devon coast, the couple are developing a new immersive restaurant experience where diners eat surrounded by the plants that created the food on their plates.

BEST ADVICE WE WERE GIVEN

'I think it's important not to listen to too much advice from other people and to think for yourself. It's ok to make things up a bit as you go along.'

ADVICE WE'D GIVE

'Community is everything in the countryside. It's vital to include and reach out to the people around you.'

How to make a fresh start

Cathy D'Arcy
Sudbury, Suffolk

Having lived in London for 35 years, Cathy needed a change; now, she has found herself a tight-knit community in a creative town

When ceramicist Cathy D'Arcy declared she was 'done with London' after living in Crouch End for nearly four decades, she was convinced it was rural space and tranquillity that she was after. Her marriage had broken down, her children had left home and she wanted to start afresh, somewhere completely different to where she'd been before. But after a stint in 'the middle of nowhere' in Suffolk, she soon realised that she also needed company and, even more importantly, culture.

'Moving back to London was never on the cards but I realised pretty quickly that I needed to feel modernity and creativity around me and to be able to walk to a shop,' says Cathy. Sudbury, where she now lives, wasn't somewhere she previously knew – but she had a friend there and it had a theatre, a couple of galleries and a good train line back to London so she could easily visit her children and grandchildren. 'It ticked the boxes,' as she says.

She packed up her rural farmhouse and swapped

'Here, you're looking for activities and ways to meet people, so you do things you'd never have done before.'

it for a modern cottage, just off Sudbury's market square. 'Getting to know the cultural scene here was almost immediate. I put feelers out for a drawing class and the next evening, a lady just turned up and knocked on my door,' Cathy says, with a grin. 'That would never have happened in north London. I knew from that moment that I was going to like it here.'

And it didn't just stop at drawing classes. Since Cathy moved to Sudbury, she has taken up print-making, after a course at the nearby print workshop, gliding, after a friend convinced her to join the local club, and voluntary gardening at a woodland refuge for people with special needs – not to mention the countless Scrabble and card-game evenings that she either hosts or is invited to. 'Here, you're filling your time in a different way – looking for activities and ways to meet people – so you do things you'd never have done before,' she explains, before adding: 'Although I draw the line at wild swimming; that's not for me.'

Despite my insistence that she is missing out on bonding with fellow swimmers during an icy plunge, Cathy has certainly found her network here. She now brands herself a 'Suffolk artist,' which gives her a

sense of place and comfort in a way that London never did. 'I've got more friends than I've ever had in my life here,' Cathy says. 'Although oddly they're all women. Sudbury, as it turns out, is full of old, friendly, fun women – which is great, for me.'

With her new social life in full swing, Covid came as a shock. 'Being on my own for lockdown was horrid but I had my garden, my pottery and my WhatsApp groups to keep me going,' Cathy says. She also took up other, more solitary, home-based pursuits such as making rag rugs and 1,000-piece jigsaw puzzles. Now, with a return to gathering, Cathy is looking forward to her games nights reforming, hosting a new still-life drawing class in her studio, and having her grandchildren to stay: 'They love it here, and this house with the garden and open-plan space is perfect for looking after them.' Does she think she'd have found so many new interests, had she stayed in London? 'Probably not, but I do miss my children and my grandchildren, so it is still a huge dilemma whether I should be here or go back to London. But I am happy here, so I feel like it's got to be the right decision, for now at least.'

Cathy has turned the living room of her
home into an open-plan ceramics studio.

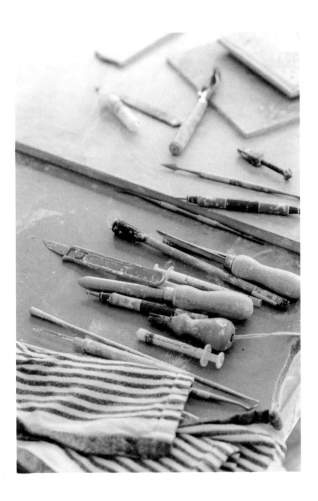

Cathy now volunteers at a local charity who organise woodland activities for people with special needs.

THE BEST ADVICE I WAS GIVEN

'My father, who was an architect, said to make sure you enjoy how you earn your living; it makes you so much more resistant to the punches life may throw at you. My pottery and my studio cheer me up every day.'

ADVICE I'D GIVE

'If you're unsure about leaving London, don't move too far away. London is always there and it becomes an even more exciting and special place to visit when you don't live there.'

How to move on a budget

Hannah & David
Faversham, Kent

When staying in London became a financial
impossibility, this family found a savvy way to
make an innovative home within their means

It's all very well choosing to leave London, but for
many people a move out of the city is far from
voluntary. So it was for David and Hannah Bullivant.
When the rent on their Camberwell flat was upped
out of their price range, Hannah, an interiors stylist,
and her husband David, a film director, were forced
to rethink. 'We really felt like we were being kicked
out. We weren't done with London at all,' says
David. But this get-up-and-go team decided not to

focus on what they couldn't have, and instead
grabbed the opportunity to kick-start a new slower,
simpler, wilder way of living for them and their two
children, eight-year-old Frankie and four-year-old
Auden.

We visit Hannah and David in May 2021. As we
drive through the town of Faversham in Kent and
out the other side, the houses suddenly peter out
and fields of corn stretch away, the Thames estuary

Although the family's indoor space is small, the surrounding fields give their children, Frankie and Auden, plenty of space to play.

'We really felt like we were being kicked out. We weren't done with London at all.'

spilling out to sea in the distance. We turn off into this vista and find, nestled in a nature reserve, Hannah and David's simple, stylish home: a static caravan, bought for £150, which they have spent the last year refurbishing inside and out, within their budget of £25,000.

The couple had been visiting friends in the summer of 2019 when a campfire conversation led to a deal: Hannah and David would build a guesthouse in their friends' field, and solve their rental dead-end by living in it while they worked. 'We're doing up the caravan in return for living here rent-free,' explains Hannah. 'And meanwhile, we're saving for a deposit on our own house – so come January 2023, we move on and the caravan is theirs.'

It may be a temporary housing solution, but as we're welcomed in and shown around, I note how much the space feels like a joyful, settled home; albeit a small one. While the outside is alive with 'nature's chorus' – as Hannah puts it – the inside is stripped back and uncomplicated: a large sofa that turns into a bed, a wood-burning stove, a tiny but functional kitchen and tucked-away bathroom, the odd piece of art, a seasonal flower wreath and, in the middle of it all, just enough space for their daughter, Frankie, to dance.

'Naturally, we're both hoarders,' admits Hannah. 'We used to live near Deptford Market and our flat was packed with all our vintage finds. But then we went travelling when Frankie was two years old, through Europe, and we put all our stuff in storage.

That kicked off our decluttering adventure.' The family has slowly been paring back their life's essentials ever since – clearing out the *stuff* and, in its place, making room for new opportunities. During lockdown, Hannah started her own series of online workshops, which explore how letting go of unnecessary objects can transform your outlook on life.

Meanwhile, David, who describes himself as a 'do-er', has been enjoying getting stuck into the renovation. Though he has called in contractors for some of the more specialised work, he's been doing most of it himself – teaching himself from YouTube videos, and from his mistakes. 'It's great practice and I'm learning so much for when we do finally buy our own house.' He beams as he talks about a horizon filled with hands-on projects. 'Starting with a small space like this has given me the confidence to perhaps tackle a slightly bigger one some day.'

I ask if the family won't feel sad to leave this place they've poured so much of themselves into, once it's completed. 'We will,' says Hannah. 'But it will also be exciting to see if we can buy a place of our own and where we might end up next.' And could that be back in London? 'No, I don't think so. That ship has sailed. We're not going back now,' they both agree. As we watch the sun set over the shimmering estuary, I get the feeling this family are only at the beginning of their countryside adventure and that, with some creative thinking, they'll make it work no matter the budget.

The stripped-back, uncomplicated interiors of the family's new home help them to focus on the more important things in life than 'stuff'.

'Starting with doing up a small space like this has given me the confidence to perhaps tackle a slightly bigger one some day.'

BEST ADVICE WE WERE GIVEN

'I remember a work colleague telling me: "Enjoy London while you've got it." And we did.'

ADVICE WE'D GIVE

'Be patient. It takes time to make friends and settle into the countryside. It is a culture shock. I'd say you need to give it at least a year.'

How to make your home your business

Rose & Jos
St Leonards-on-Sea, East Sussex

Finding a clever way to rent out their house
by the sea has given this intrepid couple
the means to never stop exploring

If you think buying a big house in the country means game over for any other adventures (surely all your time and money would be sucked up in endless renovations?), Rose Lam and Jos Lowette will make you think again. For this entrepreneurial couple, leaving London to buy a huge, Edwardian property in St Leonards-on-Sea was their ticket to freedom.

'This is our "forever" house, and that gives us the opportunity to do whatever we want to do and go wherever we want to go,' says Rose, as she and Jos proudly show me around their seaside home – which, come the weekends and school holidays, turns into an Airbnb, enabling the couple to head out and explore the world.

Rose and Jos bought the house in December 2020 and took only an impressive four months of lockdown to give this run-down monolith a new lease of life. They welcomed their first Airbnb guests

The couple's son Elvis (*right*) and his best friend Jordie on St Leonards Beach.

'This is our "forever" home, and that gives us the opportunity to do whatever we want to do and go wherever we want to go.'

in May 2020, while the walls were still drying. 'It was totally crazy, we were still up ladders touching up the window frames when they arrived,' Rose laughs.

Five years before this latest venture, Rose, who previously worked in HR, and Jos, a former travel consultant, swapped their two-bedroom flat in Clapton for their first four-bedroom home in St Leonards. 'We came here for a weekend and fell in love with this part of the England. Then when we started to look around, we just couldn't believe how affordable the big houses were.'

'It just all made sense,' says Jos. 'Neither of us wanted to stay in our London jobs. We love renovating houses and buying vintage furniture and we love travelling. It was just the perfect opportunity for us to combine all our passions.'

So where do they go when someone else is staying in their home? 'Well, that's the exciting bit,' says Jos. 'Wherever we fancy.' 'I'd say once or twice a month we go back to London to stay with friends,' Rose elaborates. 'We also regularly go back to Belgium to stay with Jos' family. Some weekends we just take our campervan up the road to a field and hang there, other times we go on bigger adventures. We had a wonderful trip around Scotland one summer, and a few years ago we drove down to Morocco and explored the Sahara.'

Renting out their house in this way not only gives the couple flexibility, it also means they get the best of both worlds: when they're not off exploring some far-flung destination, they get to live in the home that they love and be part of the local community.

It's Rose's savvy head for business that's made their set-up so successful, as well as her genuine desire to host and welcome people into her world. From the minute I arrive, I'm greeted as a long-lost friend. (I know Rose through my sister, but have only met her briefly a couple of times.) There's another friend of theirs currently staying with them while he's in between properties. And when Rose asks if I want to stay over, you know she genuinely means it. 'I've always wanted a big house filled with friends. I love the idea of one day, when we settle down a bit, staying put here while other people pop in and out the whole time.' She dreams of eventually taking the house off grid, growing her own vegetables in the garden and being self-sufficient.

There is certainly an 'anything's possible' vibe with these two. Come September they're off to Zanzibar for ten months, where Jos has enrolled himself in kite-surf school and Elvis will attend an international school that a friend recommended. But how does all this moving around affect family life? 'Elvis is such an easy kid like that, but I guess he has to be. I mean he's never slept more than five consecutive nights in one bed in his life,' says Jos. 'Yes, it was slightly easier when Elvis wasn't at school,' Rose admits. 'But we'll take each year as it comes and see how we go... We're definitely sticking to one kid though,' she adds, smiling.

Turning their home into an Airbnb has allowed Rose and
Jos to keep travelling, even while having a permanent base.

'We were still up ladders touching up the window frames when our first Airbnb guests arrived.'

BEST ADVICE WE WERE GIVEN

'Always be open to trying new things.'

ADVICE WE'D GIVE

'Travelling with kids every weekend may be a bit much; there should probably be a balance. But when you're used to a certain lifestyle, it can be even more exhausting and chaotic to stay put all the time.'

How to hold out for your dream home

Arcadia & Paddy
South Petherton, Somerset

After years of searching, this family thought they might never find the 'right' place to live, until a chance encounter saw them stumble across somewhere spectacular

Paddy and Arcadia Cerri looked at more than 50 houses over the course of three years, before buying the one they now live in 'by accident'. With no ties to any specific place outside of London, their decision to leave their terraced house in Shepherd's Bush, looking for more peace and space for their family, prompted an indefinite and sprawling search across the south of England. Yet never in this quest did they imagine they would end up buying a magnifi-cent seven-bedroom house in a Somerset village for the same price they sold their three-bedroom home on a busy roundabout in west London.

'I would have said yes to 48 of the 50 houses we looked at,' says Paddy, a coder who is currently working on a radical new crypto-currency. 'But Arcs just kept saying no. I think even the agents were starting to give up on us.' 'It's true,' laughs Arcadia, a self-confessed perfectionist, and an art dealer

specialising in medieval sculpture. 'I was really struggling to find a place that I could see us living in and I was starting to question whether it even existed. But then one day we were on our way back from seeing a house in Devon; a place that I knew before I even got out the car wasn't right. We had seen Yeabridge House on the market but had dismissed it, as it was way too big, way too expensive and way too near a road. But as we drove past it, we thought it would be fun to stop by. The owners were out so we snuck around the garden. I loved the look of the house and, surprisingly, the road noise was minimal. We didn't expect it to go any further, but the next day Paddy put in an offer within our budget. Incredibly, they got back to us, and before we knew it – we had bought the place!'

Whether buying Yeabridge House was 'an accident', as Arcadia puts it, or 'a brilliant, fortuitous mix of clever timing and luck,' as Paddy puts it, they both agree that moving here was exciting and daunting in equal measure. 'It was a huge undertaking and responsibility to be the new patrons of a house with such standing and history,' says Arcadia. For the most part she loved what the previous owners had done to the house and, rather than launch into heavy building work, decided to spend her time slowly working out how the four of them (the couple have two children: Clementine, six, and Indigo, three), could best use this incredible space they now found themselves living in.

A handsome Grade II-listed Georgian property, Yeabridge House has been tampered with over the years, including the addition of a large, late-Victorian extension. The house was beautifully stripped back by its previous owners (one of whom was an interior designer who discovered a unique green-painted wall behind a cabinet in the kitchen, which went on to inspire a new Farrow & Ball shade: 'Yeabridge Green'). But while the house's size and number of rooms certainly adds to its grandeur, it does make navigating the space slightly confusing, and unless you study the floorplan – which clarifies the ground floor is made up of entrance porch, reception hall, drawing room, morning room, dining hall, study, sitting room, back hall, kitchen/breakfast room, scullery, cellar and log store – it's easy to see how it would have been tricky to know which room to put the TV in when they first moved in.

'We were in search of space,' explains Arcadia, 'but not because we're a huge family or because we wanted to entertain – I wanted to create a sanctuary for the four of us to be together. For me, leaving London wasn't about finding a new social pool or being near a particular landmark or a school, it was all about finding a captivating home and garden that we could spread out and enjoy living in.'

And 'spread out' the family have. Arcadia and Paddy now have a sitting room each: Paddy's has dark walls, a billiard table and a sofa, while Arcadia's, across the hallway, fills with afternoon light and is decorated with her sculptures and record collection. Upstairs, despite the many options, the children choose to sleep in the same bedroom – but they do have a designated 'craft' room and a 'homework' room, while Arcadia is currently designing the interiors of her home office, as well as her and Paddy's bedroom suite.

'The house is a never-ending project, which I love,' says Arcadia – though I can't help but ask her if the space still feels a little overwhelming at times. 'I've got over that,' she tells me, 'but I do still feel incredibly lucky every day to be here.'

The previous owners' gardener has stayed on
to help the family tend to their new grounds.

*'I wanted to create a sanctuary
for the four of us to be together.'*

Arcadia and Paddy have kept the kitchen
in its original place at the back of the
house, creating a bright, practical place
for the family to cook and eat together.

The house's many rooms give the couple's two children,
Clementine and Indigo, plenty of space to play creatively.

*'It was a huge undertaking to be
the new patrons of a house with such
standing and history.'*

BEST ADVICE WE WERE GIVEN

'There is a different pace to everything outside of London – if you try to rush anything or anyone around here, it will just take longer.'

ADVICE WE'D GIVE

'Don't get pushed into certain interiors by friends and family who think they know best. Make your own decisions according to how you and your family want to live.'

How to build a new community

Rebecca & Chris
Bruton, Somerset

After years of high-pressure London careers,
this couple's move to a countryside town has given
them more time to make connections

In meeting the many interviewees in this book, I've become used to complicated exchanges of directions, easily missed driveways and postcode-less destinations. This was not the case when setting off to find the home of Rebecca McClelland and Chris Roberts. Not only is the gallery-filled Somerset town where they live firmly on the map as a destination for design lovers, but their home itself is the most prominent building on its High Street.

'We saw the potential in this building immediately as a business, a home and to kick-start an idea we've had for a long time, of opening a small art school,' says Chris of The Old Pharmacy, their stunning double-fronted Georgian house. Chris, director of foundation studies at Central Saint Martins, and his wife Rebecca, a photography director, uprooted their lives in London and moved with their two children to Bruton in January 2020.

REBECCA & CHRIS

Bruton is known
for its abundance
of galleries, design
shops and foodie
openings.

150

Needless to say with such big aspirations, there was work to be done. The business side of things was first on the list, and Chris and Rebecca immediately got to work renovating the building's two original retail spaces, before letting them out to renowned chef Merlin Labron-Johnson. Merlin had opened his Michelin-starred, farm-to-table restaurant Osip next door to The Old Pharmacy the year before and was quick to snap up the new spaces to create an additional café, deli and wine bar. Between these two foodie outlets, Chris and Rebecca's grand front door leads onto a narrow corridor stretching back to reveal a huge interior, which the couple are in the midst of turning into their family home.

'We do live in the thick of it,' says Rebecca, swerving out the way of a waiter carrying a box of fresh vegetables, as she greets me on the doorstep. It's a sunny Sunday morning in early June when I visit and the town's main street is buzzing; as we wait for her three-year-old daughter, Serafina, to come down (having decided she's wearing completely the wrong shoes for the photoshoot), Rebecca seems able to introduce me to every person that walks past. 'We did want a community when we moved, and we've found one. Everyone here has welcomed us in with open arms; it's a very powerful thing.'

After a brief tour of the ongoing building work, and quick intros to the guinea pigs in the garden, we head off to their son Obi's regular Sunday morning football match, played against a spectacular backdrop of the Bruton Dovecote and the surrounding Somerset hills. The walk there takes us past the High Street's boutiques, down cobbled alleys, across medieval bridges and around historic architecture; it's a persuasive tour of the town's appeal. As we meander through the streets, Rebecca tells me how 24 years of working in production for advertising agencies in the capital had left her in need of change. 'I was exhausted both physically and creatively and needed a break, but I couldn't have that in London. Moving here gave me the tools to step away. I'm

taking some time out, but intend to return to work at the end of this year.'

The idea of an art school was one her and Chris had been talking about for a while: a fun project that would make use of both of their skills and experience. There was space above The Old Pharmacy's retail outlets for an office and a studio, while a large guesthouse at the back could house visiting artists. 'We knew there was an existing creative community here, and we also knew Bruton has the power to attract creative people. We wanted to connect it all,' explains Rebecca.

When the pandemic hit however, and movement of people ceased, Chris and Rebecca's plans were put on hold. Not wanting to completely rest on their laurels, they dreamt up a lockdown project that would satisfy both their creativity and their need to connect with others: The Bruton Correspondence School. They contacted local artists, asking each of them to start a collage small enough to fit inside a regular envelope, and to send it on to another artist somewhere on the globe to add to – starting a chain of creativity. 'To date, we've had around 300 incredible collages back that have been round the world to different artists. They're all going on show at various locations across Bruton this summer. It's been a great way for us to build a creative network here, and has given us a real sense of identity,' says Chris.

Word has already started to get around about Chris and Rebecca's project, and both the Taunton Art School and Cambridge University have been in touch about the possibility of the couple running a workshop on mail-art, and the collaborative possibilities of drawing and image-making. 'I also just had a call the other day from a small art school in France that are keen to work with us. I love how news of our little project is spreading so organically,' says Rebecca. 'For the first time ever in my life, I feel far away from that London pressure to always have a master plan; instead, we're just seeing how it all unfolds.'

The couple rent out the house's original retail spaces to chef Merlin Labron-Johnson, who runs a café and deli there, selling veg grown on his own nearby allotment.

After 24 years of full-time work, Rebecca craved more
time to focus on 'life': wild swimming, taking walks in
nature and getting more involved with her kids' school.

'For the first time ever in my life, I feel far
away from that London pressure to always
have a master plan.'

*'Everyone here has welcomed us in with
open arms; it's a very powerful thing.'*

The family's weekly walk to Obi's Sunday
morning football game takes them across
the town's historic stepping stones to a pitch
overlooked by the Bruton Dovecote.

BEST ADVICE WE WERE GIVEN

'A friend told me early on to get stuck in, get involved in everything. I go running, swimming, gardening, I do volunteer work, I'm on the parent's association at the kids' school – and I'm having the best time, doing all these things I never had time to do when working full-time in London.'

ADVICE WE'D GIVE

'It's important to change your expectations. In London it's about big, dramatic things like the Olympic pool or a show at the Turbine Hall, but here it's about the small things... Like the lady who knits dolls and puts them on her garden fence for the kids to spot as they walk past.'

How to burst the London bubble

Stuart & Polly
Bungay, Suffolk

For these two ex-Londoners, leaving the city has
shown them just how much you can miss out on
if you never look beyond the capital

When the address you're given has the word
'castle' in it and no numbers, it's hard not to make
presumptions about the place. But while husband
and wife Stuart and Polly Pearson Wright do,
according to Google Maps, live in a castle, when I
arrive at their house (in actual fact a converted
17ᵗʰ-century barn), I find their 'castle' to be a ruin
that now sits as a backdrop to their garden – albeit,
a rather splendid one.

But then, presumptions are often hard to avoid
when you're moving between the country and the
city. As Stuart, Polly and I chat over a cup of tea in
the shadow of the castle ruin, Stuart, who is an artist,
confides that when they first left the capital in 2013,
he found it hard to let go of his preconceptions. 'In
the first year we moved here we had friends to stay
every weekend. You're sort of in a terror, an existen-
tial fear of not knowing anyone,' he admits. 'I guess

'There's this idea that, aside from the beauty of the British landscape, there is nothing else to excite you outside of London – which is just not true.'

there is this in-built worry that you won't meet anyone you connect with. Coming here, you realise just how ridiculous that idea is.'

In London, he tells me, he lived in an 'art-world bubble' that he never ventured out of. In Suffolk, they have widened their social circle to 'a wonderful bunch' of people from a huge range of professions; the area is full of interesting people doing innovative things. 'I have one friend, for example, who builds solar-panelled irrigation pumps, which he distributes in developing countries. Another is a dairy farmer who has diversified into making award-winning raw milk and fresh cheese, which he sells to top restaurants.'

It's been eight years since Stuart and Polly, who is a musician, decided they'd had enough of being outbid on houses in Clapton. When, back then, a Rightmove alert for 'a castle' in Suffolk that matched their criteria and budget came up, they were intrigued. They jumped in the car to go see it, and put in an offer straight away. The couple and their young son moved in the following January, and, Polly recalls, initially found themselves in for a bit of a shock: 'We were used to living on a busy city road, so the pitch black nights took some getting used to. At first, I was very scared of the barren wilderness of it all.'

They quickly got to work clearing the jungle that was then the garden, having (rather impressively) promised Stuart's cousin that they would host his wedding that same year. The interior, however, was more of a gradual process. 'We've done lots but it's a never-ending job really. We'll be forever chipping and tweaking away at the house, I imagine. Still

haven't got those curtains up,' Polly laughs. They both love going to local auctions and antique fairs, favouring pieces that are slightly dishevelled yet full of personality. With a sort of rough-luxe aesthetic, the interiors of their home are a mix of carefully sourced pieces and casual daily accoutrements. The result is a space that feels designed, but never too precious or serious; this is a home made for friends and family to get together. Or, as Stuart puts it, 'a place where kids can run off and play while grown-ups sit around and drink gin.'

Yet, as well as enjoying their home for social gatherings – they've since hosted two more friends' weddings – Polly and Stuart have also built strong connections to their local area. 'There is this idea that, aside from the beauty of the British landscape, there is nothing else to excite you outside of London – which is just not true,' says Polly. 'Norwich is half an hour from here and it's a great city, hugely underrated. It's got beautiful architecture, lots of independent businesses, art galleries, a lovely cinema, restaurants – and you can walk everywhere. There's also Cambridge fairly nearby, another wonderful place for culture, and Colchester has a great gallery that we often go to.'

'And there's Great Yarmouth,' Stuart adds excitedly, telling me about the 'architectural triumph' that is the town's Hippodrome Circus, a purpose-built venue and one of only three in the world with a circus floor that sinks into a pool. 'The shows there are phenomenal and have been hugely inspiring to my work,' he enthuses. 'There is a real history and beauty in these places, if you only bother to scratch the surface.'

Stuart and Polly have filled their home with objects that have a history, making the space feel eclectic and full of stories.

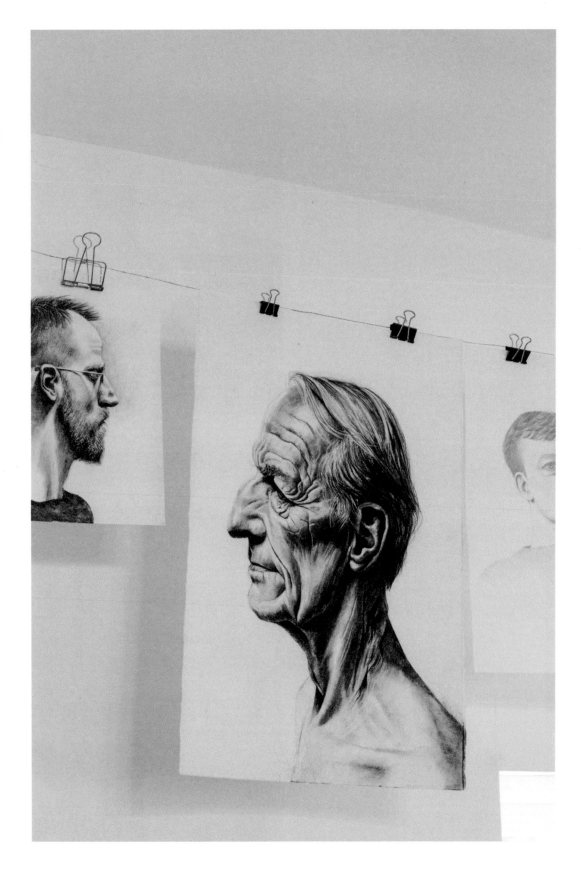

Now that Stuart's art studio is part
of his home, he can work long hours
and still put the children to bed.

The couple's new home has the feel of a smallholding: part of the castle ruin serves as a chicken coop, while Polly has reared their two sheep, Babette and Teapot, from lambs.

'We were used to living on a busy city road, so the
pitch black nights took some getting used to. At first,
I was very scared of the barren wilderness of it all.'

BEST ADVICE WE WERE GIVEN

'Learn to drive. You can't really live
in the countryside without being able
to drive.'

ADVICE WE'D GIVE

'Avoid moving out of London in the dead
of winter – the darkness and the silence
can be quite challenging at first. It'll be a
much easier transition in the summer.'

How to reset your priorities

Sally & Paul
Bildeston, Suffolk

When Sally first moved out of Hackney she thought she'd made a terrible mistake, but letting go of her London life made her reappraise what's important

I'm a firm believer that change is a good thing; that people who question things and keep their lives moving forwards often end up happier than those who continue with the same old daily grind, year after year. I found a fellow devotee to this sentiment in Sally Emslie, who, after nearly 20 years of living in London, moved with her husband, Paul Mackenzie, and their two children to a small village in Suffolk, for exactly this reason.

'London is still my favourite place on Earth, but I needed a change of scene: I needed to try something new. I actually feel quite unsettled when I don't have change around me,' Sally explains, as she welcomes me into her astonishing home: a grand, crumbling Georgian dame right in the middle of Bildeston's central square. Originally from South Africa, Sally moved to London in 2003. After an illustrious career in investment strategy, travelling

'London is still my favourite place on Earth, but I needed a change of scene.'

the world and working for clients including Google, Yahoo and Nokia, she left the corporate world in 2018 to found her own business, Manifesto Woman: a tightly curated lifestyle store where everything is second hand. She's currently got plans to open a plant-based café-meets-shop with sustainability at its core in Suffolk. We meet in March 2021, when Sally has just recently had planning permission through for major restoration work to their property. This will mean her and her family moving out and renting a cottage down the road for the best part of 18 months; it's pretty clear Sally didn't move to the countryside to put her feet up.

'I love the project, I love the adventure of it,' Sally says, talking me through some of the ambitious building work she and Paul have planned, including a sustainable heating system and large kitchen garden. I can't help wonder how, as someone who enjoys living life in the fast lane, she's found the pace of rural Suffolk since she arrived in the summer of 2019.

'I admit, for the first three months I was really struggling, and, if it wasn't for Paul calming me down and telling me to give it some more time, I may well have headed back to the city. Everything was so new, so different. The culture shock of moving can be huge. I desperately missed under-standing and being in control of what was going on around me.' Like what? 'Well, there were the small things – like I was convinced I was going to die every

time I got in a car, the roads are ridiculously narrow and people drive so fast down them. To the bigger things, like how much of my identity was wrapped up in being a Londoner and how I'd have to shift my priorities to fit in.'

A few months in, Sally made a decision: rather than miss her London self, she was going to move on and start enjoying where she was right now. For her, it was about resetting what was important and finding new hobbies: walking, paddle-boarding and trawling car-boot sales.

'In one sense I'm totally the same, but in another I'm really different from the person I was when we moved. But that's the by-product of change and I love that. It gives you a new perspective.' What's been the most positive change? 'I love that my friendship circle here is so much more all-encompassing. I never had my opinions challenged in London because all my friends dressed, ate and thought the same as me. Here we're all very different and it's truly delightful. One of my best friends here is in her 70s. Plus, I still see all my London friends, but they come and stay for the whole weekend and our relationship is all the richer for it.'

And what does she miss most? 'Oh, the usual stuff. Good Asian food, good coffee, a good late night going from bar to bar. But that's the point, these days I really enjoy missing them. That's the reset button kicking in.'

*'In one sense I'm totally the same, but in
another I'm really different from the person
I was when we moved.'*

The family's home is in the middle of Bildeston village square, and Sally loves the feeling of living right in the heart of the local community.

The couple are about to embark on a major restoration of their home, which will include adding a sustainable heating system and a kitchen garden.

'I love that my friendship circle here is so much more all-encompassing. I never had my opinions challenged in London.'

The family have always been outdoorsy, and can now take regular walks together in the countryside around their home.

BEST ADVICE WE WERE GIVEN

'Countryside living isn't always perfect, but it's worth pushing through for those moments when it really does feel like you live on holiday.'

ADVICE WE'D GIVE

'Be prepared: what you save on coffees and Ubers, you will spend double, at least, on heating and gardening equipment.'

How to find space to think

Sarah Kaye Rodden
Brasted, Kent

Artist Sarah used to think her creativity came
from city life, now she finds spending time in
nature leaves her more inspired than ever

If there was a *Family Fortunes*-style top answer as to
why people leave London, 'more space' would be it.
For Sarah Kaye Rodden, who left a two-bedroom
maisonette in Battersea six years ago for the village
of Brasted, finding a studio space and more room for
her family was the major, 'if not only', reason for
moving. But what Sarah didn't realise until later was
that more than *physical* space, it was really headspace
that she craved.

'London can be very distracting,' she explains.
'I didn't realise it when I was in the city but as an
artist it can be all too much, too intimidating.
It wasn't until we left that I found the space to take
a step back and think.' Which is exactly how I find
Sarah: calmly stepping back from her vintage drawing
board, the sun streaming through into her studio.

The house – once a print factory, then an
antiques shop, before being converted into a private

'It's in these moments in the forest, surrounded by simplicity yet complexity, that I'm least distracted and I have my clearest thoughts.'

residence by its previous owner – sits on the village high street. Her studio is on the original shop floor, and as we chat, people passing by wave to her through the large windows, while cars regularly park up and drive off outside. 'I love it being busy and the feeling of people around me, I'd feel isolated without it,' says Sarah. Her move to the countryside was never a quest for solitude or simplicity. 'I needed a space to fit my drawing board,' she jokes semi-seriously.

A self-confessed arranger and re-arranger, upstairs every corner of Sarah's home has its own curated little installation of found objects and heirlooms. Dinosaur fossils, shark's teeth and pieces of meteorite are carefully displayed, along with collections of interesting stones and bits of wood. Her own work, and that of people she admires, lines the walls – while a striking botanical sculpture by an artist friend hangs from the mezzanine. Even the dog, a charcoal-coloured lurcher, is named 4B – 'after the pencil'.

'It's not always this tidy,' Sarah assures me; her two children are at school when I visit. She describes the moments when everyone is at home: 'In one corner my son is playing Hot Wheels and has bits of

Lego strewn across the studio floor. My daughter is dancing around, and my husband John always sits right here by the window playing his guitar. It's just a perfect space for us as a family: we navigate it together.'

When it comes to her work, however, it is out in nature that she does her best thinking. Her daily walks with 4B take her through the local woods, and are a time to reset her mind and clear her head. 'I don't necessarily get inspired by natural forms, but it's in these moments in the forest, zooming into the details of the branches, appreciating the curves of the trees – surrounded by simplicity yet complexity – that I'm least distracted and I have my clearest thoughts.'

I ask if she thinks she'd still be an artist, had she stayed in London. 'My art is about observation, looking and being thoughtful. I'd like to believe that yes, I would still be working as an artist, but I genuinely feel my work wouldn't have been as clear or precise and I wouldn't have been as experimental or free-flowing with my ideas. Our move out of London has given me space to grow in every aspect of my world.'

*'London can all be too much for
an artist, too intimidating.'*

Sarah was looking for a home with enough space to
create a studio, where her beloved vintage drawing
board could take centre stage.

Her daily walks through the local woods give Sarah a chance to tune out distractions and feel inspired.

'It wasn't until we left London that I found
the space to take a step back.'

Having more space to create has
allowed Sarah to become much more
experimental in her artwork.

*'The house is a perfect space for us
as a family: we navigate it together.'*

Sarah's studio looks out over the village's high
street, and she finds the passing bustle makes
her feel less isolated while she's working.

BEST ADVICE I WAS GIVEN

'When house hunting, don't get bogged down with practicalities like en-suite bathrooms and Ofsted reports. You'll make it all work with a bit of spark and imagination.'

ADVICE I'D GIVE

'Country life really does require a good waterproof. I like a vintage military coat; I get them online from various vintage shops. They work brilliantly and just have the bits where you want the bits.'

How to get the right balance

Nicola & Andy
Charlbury, Oxfordshire

When this energetic family fulfilled their dream of heading to the Oxfordshire hills, they found staying connected to London was essential

As the saying goes, you can take a person out of the city... But does that mean you have to completely take the city out of the person? Not according to interior designer Nicola Harding, who moved with her husband Andy and their children from Shepherd's Bush to Oxfordshire in 2019. 'Truth is,' she tells me, 'while I didn't want to live in London anymore, I do love the combination of having both – more than I ever thought I would.' It's a comment that takes me a little by surprise. I've known Nicola for a number of years and her and Andy have always been resolute they would one day find a chocolate-box home in the countryside. That bit, at least, has happened as planned: their new home sits in the walled garden of a churchyard – a Cotswold-stone house through a fairytale tumbledown gate.

'I always thought I'd like to work less and get stuck into gardening and preserving stuff,' Nicola

The family's new home is in the walled garden of the local churchyard.

says, as she makes lunch for us both in her warm, comfortable kitchen. 'But maybe that's just not who I am,' she continues, explaining how leaving London hasn't given her much more time at all to focus on such wholesome hobbies; she runs her own design practice and studio, Nicola Harding & Co, with a portfolio that includes Beaverbrook hotel in Surrey, The Mitre Hampton Court and Beaverbrook Townhouse in Chelsea. 'I love taking the train in to work once or twice a week and my walk from Paddington Station to my studio is where I do so much of my thinking.' I ask if, all the same, her work-life juggle has got any easier in the countryside. 'Quite the opposite,' she replies. 'In London, work is the axis from which the rest of life rotates so it's relatively easy to fit in. Here, life is the axis around which everything rotates so you have to shoehorn work in when you can. I think this is the right way round – life should be first – but it does mean getting work done is a bit trickier.'

Andy is equally ambitious with his career and is currently the UK CEO of an Australian FinTech business. He appears in the kitchen from his home office to make a cup of tea. 'Balancing work and life certainly doesn't get any easier,' he agrees. 'But I just don't want to or need to be in London all the time. I love going in every now and then for a good dose of heady city life. Flexibility is the key: being able to consume London on your own terms.'

While the city may beckon on occasion, the couple also both recognise the importance of committing to where they live. Nicola and Andy are both active members of the village; they have made many new friends through the local school, which their youngest attends, and the local cricket club, where Andy plays every Friday evening. 'Life here is about piling back to friends' houses and the children being able to roam free,' says Nicola.

As I wander around the couple's elegant yet wonderfully personal home, I do get the sense that they have achieved their rural dream – and seemingly without any harm to their careers or their social lives. But is their life any less hectic with all this balancing to do? 'Absolutely. We live a much more peaceful, gentle life here. It's being closer to nature that calms you down and it's what I miss if I spend more than a couple of days in London,' Nicola insists, before darting off to jump on a work call in her serene garden office.

*'Life here is about piling back to friends' houses
and the children being able to roam free.'*

The house is filled with clever design features, such as the en-suite mezzanine level to the master bedroom, but ultimately feels like a cosy family home.

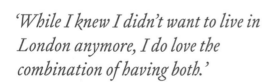

'While I knew I didn't want to live in London anymore, I do love the combination of having both.'

'I always thought I'd like to work less and get stuck into gardening and preserving stuff, but maybe that's just not who I am.'

205

BEST ADVICE WE WERE GIVEN

'We very nearly bought a bigger house that needed lots of work. A friend warned us off, saying how her parents had done just that and it had hung over them their whole lives knowing they could never quite afford to do all the work they wanted to do. A larger house that needs full renovations can quickly become oppressive.'

ADVICE WE'D GIVE

'It's so easy to get seduced by these incredible houses in the middle of nowhere, but for us having the practicality of being able to at least walk or cycle to the train station, and your kids being able to walk or cycle to see their friends, is really important.'

How to go wild

Viktor & Hannah
Sotherton, Suffolk

For this free-spirited family, leaving London for a dilapidated farm meant being able to create their own untamed utopia

When it comes to cultivating your own personal patch of wilderness in the countryside, it turns out it's not a case of simply sitting back and letting nature run riot. Artist, author and curator Viktor Wynd and his wife Hannah, an editor, moved from Hackney to a farm in Suffolk five years ago, determined to transform acres of neglected land into an idyll of flower meadows and fruit orchards. But they soon found that making their wildest dreams come true wasn't as straightforward as you might think.

'We're talking 70 to 80 years before this orchard is fully grown,' says Viktor. 'Everything here is new so it's going to take decades till it's mature.' Along with pears and apples – 'Wynd's babies', as Hannah refers to them – the current saplings also include plums, medlars, pecans, almonds, barberries, mulberries and many more curious and peculiar breeds of tree. 'It's all very exciting but it just takes

*'We have gone a bit wild
on the animal front.'*

so, so, so long,' says Hannah. 'Even to create the wild meadow naturally takes a very long time. You can plant wild flowers but they interfere with the soil and it's expensive and doesn't feel right.'

The couple made a beeline to Suffolk eight years ago, where they rented for a few years before finding this rambling Tudor farmhouse with land and outbuildings. 'It was both my and Viktor's dream to do this,' says Hannah. 'But I did have two requirements for the house... I wanted two sets of stairs. All the best houses have two sets of stairs. And it needed to be within walking distance of a pub. Going to the pub in the countryside is essential, but what's the point if you then have to drive home?'

Hannah herself lived in rural Buckinghamshire till she was seven, after which her family moved to London. However, it's her childhood memories of the countryside that are still most vivid: growing up with geese, surrounded by a bluebell wood. And it is this Eden that she's determined to give to her own children. As I arrive on a sunny Sunday morning, her three daughters are out playing with the chickens in the garden, while they excitedly await the arrival of three baby tortoises. Soren, their 15-year-old son, is in the sitting room with his pet snake, overlooked by Sheba the dog and Barnaby the cat. Peacocks, ducks and guinea fowl roam free in the garden, with donkeys and beehives in the field beyond.

The meadow may be a few years in the making, but with such a wandering menagerie of pets and livestock, it feels like they have at least one part of their utopia wrapped up. 'We have gone a bit wild on the animal front,' Hannah laughs, as she shows me around her antique gypsy caravan – a birthday present from Viktor that she intends to turn into her writing retreat. 'You just missed the miniature ponies. And my beloved pet turkey, Sweet Pea, whom I used to sing lullabies to and stroke to sleep – the fox got him just a few weeks ago. Oh, and Gilbert the hedgehog, he was everyone's favourite. He died recently, too. We had a shoebox burial planned for him, but Viktor had him stuffed.'

It's this frank, slightly eccentric, take on the country idyll – or the 'Wynd twist', as Hannah puts it – that sums up the spirit of this family. From the eggs incubating on the kitchen dresser, carefully planned to hatch at Easter, to the handmade quilts in the girls' rooms made by Granny, their home is filled with personality and devotion to Hannah and Viktor's rural dream. Does that mean this is a forever home for the Wynds? 'Yes, absolutely. We could never sell this place, we're far too invested in it. Which is a terrifying level of commitment really,' says Hannah. 'But then, the countryside makes you confront your own mortality on a daily basis. The reality is, by the time this orchard or wild meadow comes to anything, I'll be far from a young maiden. But at least the new baby tortoises will get to enjoy it.'

'I had two requirements for the house... I wanted two sets of stairs. All the best houses have two sets of stairs. And it needed to be within walking distance of a pub.'

Hannah is renovating
an antique caravan
Viktor bought her into
a writing studio in the
garden.

The family now have a menagerie of beloved pets and livestock including tortoises, chickens, donkeys and a snake.

'We could never sell this place now, we're far too invested in it. Which is a terrifying level of commitment really.'

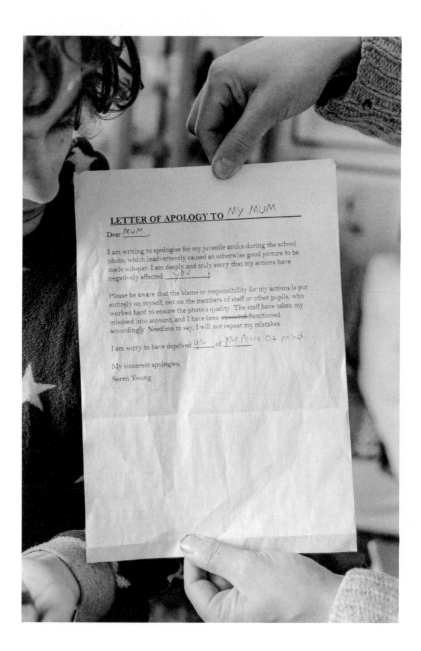

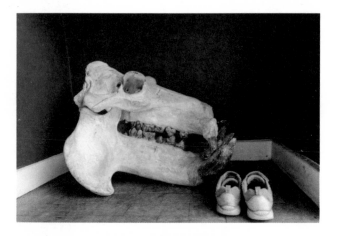

BEST ADVICE WE WERE GIVEN

'Choose your location carefully. And rent first in an area you think you might want to live in, so you get the lay of the land before you commit.'

ADVICE WE'D GIVE

'You can't add age – especially to a garden. Finding a mature garden with large trees, or a walled garden, is very special – that kind of character is so beautiful and there is no way you can add that within your lifetime.'

How to make it mean something

Steve Barron
Pidley, Cambridgeshire

When Steve left the city to live off grid, his journey into
eco-friendly living led him to something extraordinary

'I wanted to do something for the planet. I didn't quite know what, but something,' says film director Steve Barron. He's explaining to me how, in 2017, he not only embarked on building a revolutionary, carbon-capturing home in a field in Cambridgeshire, but also became a pioneering conservationist and organic hemp farmer with over 50 acres of land.

Gemma, Steve's daughter, was baffled at first: 'When my father said he was starting a hemp farm, I thought he'd lost his mind and we were in some kind of *Breaking Bad* episode,' she laughs. But, having moved back from Nairobi with her husband and two young daughters during the pandemic, Gemma and her family are now staying on the farm with her dad. 'I'm so proud of him and so happy to be a part of this beautiful thing. Plus, we get to live here,' she says, then heads out with her youngest daughter to start planting beans in the vegetable patch.

*'I wanted to do something for the planet.
I didn't quite know what, but something.'*

'It couldn't have worked out any better,' says Steve, whose quest to make a difference and leave the Earth better than he found it led him to discover the vast eco-friendly capabilities of hemp, a fast-growing strain of the cannabis plant. 'I hadn't really planned any of it, but one thing led to another and here I am, able to live here with my grandchildren, with some sort of purpose. I couldn't be happier.'

With a career that includes directing music videos for songs such as 'Take on Me' by a-ha and 'Money for Nothing' by Dire Straits, and films including *Teenage Mutant Ninja Turtles*, it's not as if Steve has had a humdrum life up till now. But listening to him wax lyrical about soil regeneration and combine harvesters, there's no doubt he's found a new passion for hemp as a material for the 21st century.

It's a passion that has brought him here: to Margent Farm in rural Cambridgeshire where, in the spring of 2017 (having been given the go-ahead by the police), he planted his first hemp seeds on a derelict dairy farm purchased with his business partner, Fawnda Denham. 'I had no idea where it was going to go, but I knew just the very act of growing hemp was pulling carbon out of the atmosphere at an extraordinary rate,' he explains. Eager to learn more about this incredible plant, Steve got in touch with nearby Cambridge University where he spoke to some of the world's experts in natural materials. The knowledge he garnered there inspired him to start experimenting with creating normally plastic-heavy products out of hemp – including trays, coasters and backpacks – which he now sells alongside oils and balms made on his farm.

Meanwhile, Steve was introduced to architect Paloma Gormley of Practice Architecture, and the idea of 'growing a house' out of the hemp fields that surrounded it started to take shape. Together, they spent the next year developing Steve's home's unique interior structure – made using prefabricated timber-framed building blocks filled with 'hemp-crete' (a mulch of hemp, lime and water). For the exterior, they developed a revolutionary cladding made from the outer coating of hemp stalks combined with resin taken from agricultural waste. Built on the footprint of an old cattle shed, the house remains entirely off grid, powered by a combination of wind turbines and solar panels, with a biomass boiler for heating.

There is no question that Steve is a remarkable conservationist, but what is so charming is the way in which he does it. Nothing is preachy or worthy. He's not obsessively calculating his own carbon footprint or worrying about the odd plastic toy in his grandchildren's playroom. He is powered entirely by his own impulse to make a difference and give his life a purpose. And, with any luck, he may just inspire others along the way.

'It really has been like a revolving door. I never had a plan and I've still got no idea where it will all lead. We've got a series of environmental talks and lunches with a collective of local growers and chefs coming up, which I'm excited about. I never intended the house to even be my home initially. And then, when my family needed a place to stay, it was perfect. It was like I built it for them, and for us to be here together. It's funny how things turn out.'

Steve's daughter, Gemma, and her family moved back to the UK from Nairobi
when the pandemic hit and are now living with Steve in his pioneering home.

'I hadn't really planned any of it, but one thing led to another and here I am: able to live here with my grandchildren, with some sort of purpose.'

Steve has turned one of the old cattle sheds
on his plot into a makeshift home office.

Steve had to be given the go-ahead
by local police to begin farming hemp,
a strain of the cannabis plant with
incredible eco-friendly potential.

BEST ADVICE I WAS GIVEN

'How to pick? Advice and lots of it, has
been essential. I'm not a farmer, nor am I
professor, scientist, architect or techni-
cian. I'm not even handy with a drill. So
along this whole process I've relied on
the help of some hugely clever folk who
really get it. It could have gone so wrong,
and yet it has all turned out so right.'

ADVICE I'D GIVE

'I find going on a hunch, with a sprinkle
of naivety, is what propels us all forwards.
Go blind and learn as you go.'

How to take your best friend with you

James & Adolfo
Deal, Kent

Adolfo hadn't planned to leave London, until his friend James pitched him a creative business idea he couldn't resist

It's one thing to up and leave London on your own. But it's a whole lot more fun if you can convince your best friend to come too. James Shouli (*pictured left*) and Adolfo Ramos Alicart, who both work in creative visual merchandising, had been friends and colleagues for over 20 years when, in 2018, James and his partner Paul made the leap to move from Crystal Palace to Deal. When, a few months later, James saw an opportunity to open a lifestyle store in his new seaside town, he knew exactly who he wanted as his business partner.

Conveniently, Adolfo and his partner Craig had bought a holiday cottage just a few miles up the coast a couple of years before, in the village of Kingsdown. The couple had no intentions of moving permanently from their home in Herne Hill however; they planned for it to be a weekend getaway that they would slowly renovate. But when James came knocking

James and Adolfo change the store around every Thursday to ensure that even their regular customers keep coming back and feeling inspired anew.

'Leaving London wasn't something I'd considered
until James showed me how possible it actually was.'

with his plan to open a store dedicated to art, craft and nature in the tucked-away gardens of Deal Castle, Adolfo was suddenly very tempted to change tack.

'Leaving London wasn't something I'd considered until James showed me how possible it actually was,' says Adolfo. 'I would see James having this wonderful life in Deal but still, with careful planning, keeping up with all his clients and friends in London. In the end I just thought, "Let's do it, let's live here."'

We're sat outside James and Adolfo's store, The Green & Found, which – aside from a two-week run just before Christmas 2020 – finally opened to the public in April 2021 as a 'sanctuary of simplicity' (and many covetable homewares). The building is a former stable block that dates back to 1806 – James stumbled upon it while searching for a studio space and, despite having fallen into severe disrepair, it sparked a yearning to do something he'd been thinking about for a long time.

'I've worked in retail all my career, so I always thought about having my own shop, but it was never going to be a high-street-boutique affair. I just found the building's history and setting totally irresistible,' explains James. 'And I knew Adolfo would, too.'

He was right. Convincing Adolfo was the easy part. English Heritage, the owners of the stable block, took longer to be won over. But after some careful negotiations, the friends finally signed a lease for the building for two years, just weeks before the pandemic forced all non-essential shops to close.

While, in hindsight, this wasn't an ideal time to launch a new business, it did allow them to concentrate fully on transforming the disused building into the plant-filled design haven it is today.

Now, the shop's warm and elegant interior showcases a meticulously curated array of products ranging from antiques to unique handmade objects, all displayed with utmost creativity and care. James and Adolfo get together every Thursday to change the space around, and make sure that everything from the lighting to the music and even the scent is just right. 'We both work in the art of display and we both love collecting things,' explains James, in reference to how much time, effort and love goes into creating the Green & Found shopping experience.

It's clear how much these two enjoy sourcing and styling, but what about being shopkeepers? Adolfo admits he had been a little nervous about this aspect of the business. His new neighbours however quickly put him at ease: 'People in Deal are so relaxed and chatty. It feels like people here want to be inspired; there's not the cynicism or the competition that you get in London.'

So are the pair hoping to persuade more of their city social circle to join them by the sea? 'A lot of them have left recently, but it was nothing to do with us,' says James. 'I think there comes a point when, you still love London, but you've just had enough – you need a bit of peace and quiet. My friends who feel like that don't need me to convince them.'

*'I just found the building's history
and setting totally irresistible.
And I knew Adolfo would, too.'*

The friends describe their store, Green & Found,
as a sanctuary of simplicity, art, craft and nature.

James and his partner Paul (*above*) now live in Deal,
while his friend Adolfo and partner Craig (*right*) have
moved to the village of Kingsdown, just up the coast.

*'It feels like people here want to be inspired;
there's not the cynicism or the competition
that you get in London.'*

Adolfo had worked in visual merchandising for many years, and his aesthetic eye is apparent in his tranquil new home near Kingsdown Beach.

BEST ADVICE WE WERE GIVEN

'I was worried that I was a bit young
to leave London and settle by the coast.
But I remember someone telling me
when we first moved that you come
to Deal to live, not to die. I like that.'

ADVICE WE'D GIVE

'Just do it, just move... It'll be fine.'